Always Sisters

Alda Ellis

WITH HOLLY HALVERSON

HARVEST HOUSE PUBLISHERS

EUGENE, OREGON

Always Sisters
Copyright ©1998 Harvest House Publishers
Eugene, Oregon 97402

Library of Congress Cataloging-in-Publication Data
Ellis, Alda,1952-
    Always sisters / Alda Ellis.
        p. cm.
    ISBN 1-56507-896-9
    1. Sisters I. Title.
HQ759.95.E43 1998   98-14675
306.875'4—dc21   CIP

Design and production by Left Coast Design, Portland, Oregon

Artwork which appears in this book is from the personal collection of Alda Ellis.

Scripture quotations are from the Holy Bible, New International Version®.
Copyright ©1973, 1978, 1984 by the International Bible Society.
Used by permission of Zondervan Publishing House.

Printed in China
98 99 00 01 02 03 04 05 06 07 / IM / 10 9 8 7 6 5 4 3 2 1

BIBLIOGRAPHY

Curie, Eve. *Madame Curie: A Biography.* New York: Garden City Publishing, 1943.

Gish, Lillian with Ann Pinchot. *The Movies, Mr. Griffith and Me.* Englewood Cliffs, NJ: Prentice-Hall, Inc., 1969.

Halperin, John. *The Life of Jane Austen.* Baltimore, MD: The John Hopkins University Press, 1984.

Sewall, Richard B. *The Life of Emily Dickinson, Volumes 1 & 2.* New York: Farrar, Straus and Giroux, 1974.

Wilder, Laura Ingalls. *Little Town on the Prairie.* New York: Harper & Row, 1941.

Zochert, Donald. *Laura: The Life of Laura Ingalls Wilder.* New York: Avon Books, 1976.

Dedicated to Cheryl

The days of handing down a favorite
sweater or a favorite toy are well behind us.
Days or even weeks may pass without us talking,
and then the phone rings. It is as if time stood still,
and it was only yesterday—and we are there for each
other. You are always in my prayers, forever in
my heart. Thank you for always being there.

Your sister,
Alda

Contents

My sister! With that thrilling word
Let thoughts unnumbered wildly spring!
What echoes in my heart are stirred,
While thus I touch the trembling string.

MARGARET DAVIDSON

For many women the thought of a treasured sister does indeed create "echoes in the heart." Friends can be close, but none so close as one who shares your history, lineage, legacy. When delight arrives and dreams take shape, who better to shout gladness with than a sister? And when life's clouds gather, who better to understand one's particular pains and to soothe her stings? Blest be the tie that balms. . . .

The poignantly close sisters in this book all shared the pangs of disappointment and the heavenly heights of joy. In these stories the presence of a sister sometimes meant the difference between giving up and going on—and often resulted in benefits felt worldwide. Lavinia Dickinson provided a protected haven in which her sensitive sister Emily could produce some of America's finest poems. Jane Austen needed her sister Cassandra for simple, ongoing conversation; friends came too hard for her. Were it not for Marie Curie's sister Bronya, she may never have discovered what would become a life-saving substance: radium. Laura Ingalls helped ensure her sister Mary's education at a college for the blind, and Dorothy and Lillian Gish shared the rigors of the acting profession in a kinship so strong that their truest center was with each other.

I was ten years old when my mother gave me the gift of a sister. While some sisters are kindred spirits from the very beginning, I really began to appreciate my sister years later. We had the usual days of fussing over a Barbie doll, of crying over a ruined mohair sweater, of listening in on a boyfriend's conversation. But maybe it was the handing down of my room when I left home, or perhaps the moment she stood as the maid of honor at my wedding (and I at hers) that polished our bond of friendship like no other. And now that our mother is gone, I have come to realize what a precious gift a sister truly is.

My sister took a quieter road than I did, as a nurse, wife, and mother. In my mother's failing days I saw my sister shine and take charge. With enormous appreciation for gifts and talents I did not possess, I saw my sister in a new light. She had always quietly been there, right beside me, but most of the time in my shadow. How blessed I felt that God had given me a sister who was not only a shoulder to lean on, but who could take the lead when I was unable. My sister will always have a special place in my heart.

I have you in my heart...

THE BOOK OF PHILIPPIANS

$\mathcal{F}$ or there is
no friend like a sister,

In calm or stormy weather,

To cheer one on the tedious way,

To fetch one if one goes astray,

To lift one if one totters down,

To strengthen whilst one stands.

CHRISTINA ROSSETTI

My Sister, My Heroine

Laura and Mary Ingalls

Long before she captivated the world with her accounts of the frontier life in the Little House books, Laura Ingalls Wilder lived them. On the wild prairies of South Dakota, when Laura was but a young teenager, she forged a role she could never have predicted and would never have chosen: that of heroine for her older sister Mary.

In 1879, scarlet fever attacked the Ingalls household and left Mary—beautiful, good, intelligent Mary—blind. From that time on, Pa Ingalls instructed, Laura was to be

Mary's eyes on the world. She would describe every detail of expression and color, so Mary could picture it too. With Laura at her side as both teacher and guide, Mary would miss nothing.

Though it was an assignment Laura accepted eagerly, she and Mary had not always been amiable companions. As a child Laura envied Mary's golden hair (her own was "a dirt-colored brown"), her seemingly effortless piety, her ability to keep clean. It just seemed to Laura that hard things came easily to Mary.

Yet once sickness had stolen the sight from Mary's

clear blue eyes, nothing came easily to her. Her beloved studies halted, Mary was dependent, helpless, needy in a way Laura never imagined. And she submitted herself to do all she could to ease her sister's suffering.

As Laura formed word-pictures of the world, read her own school lessons aloud so Mary could keep up, and became her sister's companion on walks across the endless prairie, her old resentments melted into admiration. Even in the face of loss and disappointment, Mary blossomed. Strolling together one day, Laura noticed Mary's acceptance of what life had given her.

"There Mary stood in the midst of the green and flowery miles of grass rippling in the wind, under the great blue sky and white clouds sailing, and she could not see. Everyone knows that God is good. But it seemed to Laura that Mary must be sure of it some special way."

News reached the Ingalls family of a college for the blind in Iowa, and a dream was born. Mary, who so loved to learn, must go. When the high price of tuition was discussed, Laura naturally decided to contribute all she could. It was a decision that would cost her more than money.

Laura accepted a job in town, away from her snug

and friendly home on the prairie, sewing men's shirts in a shop full of tension and quarrels. The first day, as she walked with Pa to town, Laura threw off the "trembly feeling" she had about working for strangers and shouldered her commitment to Mary. Working from sunup to sundown, earning a meager $1.50 per week, Laura eventually added nine dollars to Mary's college fund.

> *And do not forget*
> *to do good and to share with others...*
>
> THE BOOK OF HEBREWS

The fund filled slowly, but the time came when Mary's tuition was collected. Next came the cost Laura felt most deeply: Mary would move away, for years at a time. Laura couldn't imagine life without her, and tears choked their conversation on their last walk together. Laura glanced about their home, and read the sunset for Mary: "The sun has gone through the white clouds. It is a huge, pulsing ball of liquid fire. The clouds above it

are scarlet and crimson and gold and purple, and the great sweeps of cloud over the whole sky are burning flames."

And then, Mary was gone. The stillness pained Laura, but the Ingalls rejoiced in Mary's progress at college. She thrived and Laura was soon distracted from her loss by a teaching job, a suitor, and growing up.

While it's certain Laura would never deem her actions as "heroic," by any definition, they were. Her sacrifices sprang from a heart of love, and perhaps most unexpected of all, Laura became as "truly good" as ever she saw her strong and beautiful sister.

You can't think how I depend upon you, and when
you're not there the colour goes out of my life...

VIRGINIA WOOLF

*S*ome people make your

life more wonderful

than you ever

thought it would be.

ANONYMOUS

My Sister, My Safe Harbor

Emily and Lavinia Dickinson

Their Amherst, Massachusetts, home was filled with wit, intelligence, and turbulent emotion, their lives with joy and tragedy. Thus Emily and Lavinia (Vinnie) Dickinson were sources of solace for one another. Particularly for the sensitive and high-strung poet, a harbor of safety was most necessary.

Though Emily loved her parents devotedly, she seemed never to feel their parental closeness. Rather she leaned on Vinnie, her closest companion for over fifty

years. Indeed she even wrote a friend that "[Vinnie] has no Father and Mother but me and I have no Parents but her." No complaints accompanied this remark, but it reflects Emily's sentiment that her parents were less bound to her heart than was Vinnie. It is true that Vinnie took great pride in her sister's genius, a trait seemingly lost on the rest of the family.

Vinnie herself leaned into her role as family caretaker. Of the brooding, often serious siblings, Vinnie was "leaven"—the practical, uncomplicated member who balanced the whole. In a family rich in intellectual resources, Vinnie was equally colorful, bold, and honest. What she lacked in lyrical ability she made up for in loyalty, and Emily was not the only one who benefited from her affection.

Yet perhaps Emily appreciated Vinnie's care the most. She felt most easy with Vinnie, protected from the world she increasingly avoided and even from the household demands that might divert her energies from more poetic pursuits. To a friend who had just lost his brother, Emily described Vinnie as her "Soldier and Angel" who carried "a 'drawn Sword' in behalf of Eden." She added in her letter, "Your bond to your brother reminds me of mine to my sister— early, earnest, indissoluble. Without her life were fear, and Paradise a cowardice, except for her inciting voice."

Vinnie respected Emily's need for an Eden and she guarded it well. Emily's eventual, complete withdrawal into the Amherst Homestead becomes more understandable in light of Vinnie's contribution. Why venture out when all she needed was within? As Emily absorbed herself in privacy, except for family, Vinnie minimized her "disappearance" as an action less bizarre than inconsequential: it was "only a happen." She further

pooh-poohed Emily's growing reputation as a spinster who, after a broken heart, retired from public life. She saw instead the poet's need to live a sheltered life, devoted to her nieces, nephews, friends, and work—and Emily recognized the favor.

Vinnie never shone more than when crisis struck the Dickinson household. Both Emily and her brother, Austin, found deaths in the family overwhelming, nearly mortal wounds. When the Dickinson patriarch, Edward, died, Emily recovered behind closed doors and Austin huddled alone in his pain. Vinnie organized the mourning and aimed them toward healing. After a nephew's death, Emily was ill for weeks with a "nervous shock"; her grieving brother was

similarly prostrate. It was Vinnie who comforted, who contacted friends, who drove despair from the house. No wonder Emily said of her relationship with her sister, "Vinnie has been all, so long, I feel the oddest fright at parting with her for an hour, lest a storm arise, and I go unsheltered."

The vital tie between the Dickinsons had perhaps its finest moment after Emily's death in 1886. The sisterly allegiance that burned so brightly through Emily's life led Vinnie to pursue with tenacity the publication of Emily's poems. Since others in the Dickinson clan either missed or misunderstood Emily's talent, without Vinnie's insistence the world may never have known the joyous, brilliant poetry of the Belle of Amherst. In this way Emily's safe harbor launched the ship of her dreams: the recognition of the world she so little encountered.

I would like more sisters, that the taking out
of one, might not leave such stillness.

EMILY DICKINSON

Our relationship was simple as breath, complex as circulation. She was only the first person I could tell the truth to.

ELIZABETH FISHEL

My Sister, My Faithful Friend

Jane and Cassandra Austen

O ne wonders if Cassandra Austen chuckled in delight at the birth of her sister, Jane. In a family rich in sons, Jane's appearance must have been a beacon. Yet had Cassandra known the prickles she would endure with her beloved but difficult female sibling, she may have sighed instead.

Jane would never be an easy companion. From an early age she was cynical, critical, opinionated. As a single woman in a society that celebrated marriage and family, Jane suffered from the expectations of her times. Adding to her

burden was a lack of finances that dogged the Austen family over years. Until successful publication of her books, including *Sense and Sensibility* and *Pride and Prejudice*, Jane's mind was ever at unrest considering expenses.

It makes sense, then, that in the Austen household of six brothers and two sisters, Cassandra and Jane shared a bedroom—all their lives. It is telling that even as the household diminished, Jane and her sister kept close quarters. They did the same emotionally.

> *Love always protects, always trusts, always hopes, always perseveres. Love never fails.*
>
> THE BOOK OF 1 CORINTHIANS

Though separated for months at a time, the two wrote numerous letters keeping each other up to date on dances, relatives, illnesses, male suitors (or the lack thereof), and sentiments regarding the doings of every person in their family. What Cassandra provided for Jane was a powerful resource: constant, though often written, communication. An eager ear. Acceptance.

Jane's thoughts were radical for her day. She believed in marriage for love alone, not just financial security or society's approval. She wrote for publication when professional women writers were held suspect. Flouting the traditional view of a

woman's role as one of unquestioning loyalty to family and friends, Jane chose instead to be unique—to be herself. She wrote her sister once, "If I am a wild Beast, I cannot help it." It is clear Jane valued sincerity over sympathy, "hardness to softness, sense to sensibility."

In Cassandra, though, Jane's bristling personality found an evidently willing comrade. Cassandra herself never married and served her sister, as well as the rest of her family, devotedly. She was apparently immune to Jane's barbs—or

at least, took no long-standing offense to them—and remained Jane's best friend faithfully, if not cheerfully. Though Cassandra was seemingly more traditionally minded than Jane, one wonders if she wasn't inspired by Jane's originality and strength of character in a world where women were considered weak and incapable.

Additionally bonding the two women was their mutual disappointment in love. First Cassandra and years later, Jane, met men they respected and hoped to marry, but their dreams were quelled by both young men's premature deaths. For Jane, who attached herself to few, and then to those fervently, the loss was especially deep. No doubt Cassandra's presence and understanding of her grief brought needed compassion and hastened healing.

Surprisingly it was Jane, the headstrong and sturdy sister, whose health failed first. Tuberculosis made her its victim and slowly stole away her life. Over Jane's last months Cassandra faithfully tended Jane and stayed close; Jane praised her gentle care. "Cassandra is such an excellent Nurse, so assiduous and unwearied!" "Words fail me in any attempt to describe what a Nurse [Cassandra] has been to me." Cassandra—"tender, watchful, indefatigable"— "what I owe to her . . . I can only cry over it." In return for these loving (and lifelong) services, just before her death Jane gave her sister the gift she herself waited long in life to receive: financial relief. In her will she left Cassandra nearly everything she owned.

Cassandra was close to Jane to the end. While Jane lay on her deathbed, her head rested on a pillow on her sister's lap. Jane died in Cassandra's arms on July 18, 1817, at the age of forty-one.

For her part, Cassandra felt her bereavement in the singular way one would expect of Jane's best and essential friend. Austen family members noted to one another that no one grieved as Cassandra did; truly she alone seemed to celebrate the diamond behind the rough in Jane Austen. After her death Cassandra said, "She was the sun of my life . . . the gilder of every pleasure, the soother of every sorrow . . . It is as if I had lost a part of myself. I loved her only too well, not better than she deserved."

But we must stem the tide of malice, and pour into the wounded bosoms of each other, the balm of sisterly consolation.

MARY BENNET
Pride and Prejudice

She is a bowl

of golden water

which brims

but never overflows.

VIRGINIA WOOLF

My Sister, My Home

Lillian and Dorothy Gish

Lillian and Dorothy Gish embarked upon auspicious acting careers at the tender ages of five and four, respectively. As they grew into roles in the theater and later in silent pictures, their connection formed the foundation of what would be, along with their mother, their only true family. The Gish sisters lost the company of their father while they were still very young, and their mother never remarried. Dorothy's own marriage faltered, and Lillian remained single all her life. The Gishes formed a familial triangle whose bonds were all the home they ever needed.

It was a home full of motherly provisions—"serenity and love." There the sisters, alike in talent yet different in nearly every other aspect, flourished. In their acting endeavors they knew as friends people most respect as legends: Mary Pickford, Noel Coward, Ronald Colman, John Gielgud. In off-screen life, each sister's differences rallied to complete the other. Lillian loved her work; Dorothy loved her play. Dorothy was carefree; Lillian was melancholy. In the ocean, Lillian swam; Dorothy splashed. Dorothy's cheer was a source of envy for her sister, who remarked, "She takes nothing seriously but her mother, her meals and her dog. . . . I want to be like she is."

Yet Dorothy's admiration of Lillian was as strong. "She remains steadfast, unshaken, imperturbable. . . . I wish with all my heart I could see my life so clearly, so wholly, so free from confusion and march with such firm vigor toward achievement."

And "march with vigor" was what
Lillian did, winning glorious reviews and graduating, when the time came, into "talkies." Whatever
medium she performed in, she conquered. Dorothy's
career bloomed as well. Her playfulness earned her
roles as actress and as comedienne, parts her ebullient
manner suited her for perfectly. Lillian noticed that
whenever Dorothy arrived at a gathering, "the party
began." Yet her cheerful spirit belied a personality troubled by self-doubt and anxiety—which made her need
Lillian even more.

Indeed, Dorothy loved her home. When Lillian
contracted Spanish influenza, Dorothy hovered in the
sickroom, trying to absorb the germs so she wouldn't be
sent away for the duration of Lillian's recovery. Even after
her marriage Dorothy had to be persuaded by her mother
to live with her husband. "If I'd thought you would put
me out, I wouldn't have married," she declared tearfully.
It was a mercy that the Gish family ties remained powerful, so that when Dorothy's marriage ended she still had a
place—and people—to call home.

Lillian endured her own troubles. One businessman

cheated and hassled her for years with baseless lawsuits. Another man, whose proposals Lillian refused, threatened to harm her or himself. There were even kidnapping scares from a stranger. Also to be coped with were difficult films, the sad decline of the Gishes' mentor, director D. W. Griffith, and eventually their mother's stroke and death. Though their work kept the women frequently apart, a special sense connected them even across distances. Lillian and Dorothy maintained their link, saw one another whenever possible, and were comforted by each other's presence.

As the years passed, Lillian, despite her fragile appearance, was as strong as she was successful. Dorothy wasn't. Stomach problems plagued her for years, and pneumonia finally felled her, with Lillian at her bedside, in 1968. Lillian continued to work until she was in her nineties.

The women had written of each other: "Dear darling Dorothy . . . is the side of me that God left out. . . . She is like 'a bright flag flying in the breeze.'" Lillian "is a never-ending source of astonishment. . . . I never cease to wonder at my luck in having for my sister the woman who, more than any other woman in America, possesses all the qualities of true greatness." The love reflected in those statements, written when the Gish ladies were young but relished for a lifetime, was what made their mutual home a sweet one.

> *The love that grew with us from our cradles*
> *never knew diminutions from time or distance.*
> *Other ties were formed, but they did not supersede*
> *or weaken this. Death tore away all that was mortal*
> *and perishable, but this tie he could not sunder.*

CHARLOTTE ELIZABETH TONNA

In thee my soul

shall own combined

The sister and the friend.

CATHERINE KILLIGREW

My Sister, My Heart's Comfort

Marie Curie and Bronya Dluska

Marie Curie, a startlingly bright child born in Russia-oppressed Poland, early lost track of time and atmosphere in her love of books. Despite her fascination with study and her eventually obsessive—yet historic—work in science, Marie never lost track of—or need for—her elder sister Bronya.

Bronya's influence established itself largely after the death of the girls' mother. Long suffering from tuberculosis, Marie's mother always held herself at a distance from her family lest she infect them with her affliction. When she

died, Bronya became the warm, mothering presence Marie had always longed for. Throughout the passionate, remarkable phases of Marie's seemingly inexhaustible work, she leaned on Bronya in her darkest moments.

A tie that bound them closely, as members of the underground intelligentsia in Poland, was a demanding love of country. Both sisters believed in and worked toward their own education as a means of strengthening their homeland through their eventual teaching of others. As household burdens fell increasingly on Bronya—their professor father spent all his energy providing for the

family—Marie worried about her sister's sparkling, though dormant gifts. Bronya's dreams lay in Paris schooling, a degree in medicine, and a country practice in their beloved Poland. Out of her concern, Marie strategized a plan by which Bronya might realize her longings: Marie would hire herself out as a household servant, earning enough funds to support, with their father's help, Bronya's schooling. And one day, after she had worked and saved enough, Marie too would go to school.

Awed at Marie's sacrifice, Bronya hesitantly accepted the plan and moved to France. Marie found herself attached as governess to a disagreeable family. Though devotion to her sister drove her on, she weakened in the face of the crude and snobbish people who employed her. Complicating Marie's unhappiness was her employers' rejection of her as fiancée for their son, with whom Marie had fallen in love. The parents felt her too low in society; she was worthy to teach, but that was all. Separation from her family also wracked her and slowly, Marie's own dreams died.

After years of "prison"—or so Marie

deemed her confinement to domesticity—destiny, in the form of Bronya, took a hand. The older sister finally found some financial means of support; she not only refused further funds from Marie, she began to pay her back . . . and she concocted Marie's means of escape. Soon to marry, Bronya invited Marie to come to Paris to take up her studies—she could live with her and her husband. Marie was discouraged to the point of despair: "My heart is so black," she wrote Bronya. Yet circumstances swerved and Marie's vivacity returned. She contacted her sister, who renewed her offer, and Marie's distinguished career began with her studies at the Sorbonne.

Marie's daughter Eve was to write later, "Between Marie and Bronya a magnificent romance had been unfolding for years past: the romance of sacrifice and devotion, of mutual help." This sisterly romance was expressed in ways never trivial, always deep. Bronya and her husband Casimir shared their home with Marie. When she embarked to study and live alone, she starved herself to accommodate costs; Bronya and Casimir found her fainting and restored her health. Marie, distracted by her scientific fascination, relied upon her sister in the strange city for common sense,

for companionship, for affection.

Marie and her colleague, fellow scientist Pierre Curie, eventually made their greatest discoveries in each other, and married. Immediately and joyfully swallowed by their ravenous appetites for research, Marie and Pierre spent long and late hours at work. Yet Bronya never lost her place as favored friend. As Marie's work progressed and she began to suspect the existence of "new matter"— soon to be recognized as polonium and radium—it was

to Bronya that she confided her news. When Marie finally stopped researching long enough to pursue her doctorate, Bronya attended the exams. And after the difficult birth of Marie's daughter Eve, ever-faithful Bronya calmed with her presence and scattered peace where melancholy ruled.

Not surprisingly, when Bronya and her family eventually moved back to Poland to found a sanitorium, Marie wrote her plaintively: "You can't imagine what a hole you have made in my life."

The hole became a yawning chasm. Marie and Pierre succeeded in isolating the new substances and astonishing the scientific community. They worked feverishly on their discoveries, produced two children, and enjoyed a profound marital and professional union. When Pierre was killed in an accident in 1906 and Marie left a widow at age thirty-eight, Bronya, of course, came immediately. And as Marie suffered in her grief, Bronya was among those who fought for her place as successor in Pierre's research. Consequently Marie was the first woman ever awarded such a position in higher education in France.

In those confusing, horrible days, it was Bronya whom Marie called to witness her final act of grief: the disposal of Pierre's bloody clothes. Reluctant to part with the last remnants of her husband, Marie had to have the clothes pried from her hands and tossed into the fire. At last she confessed, "I could not have endured having this touched by indifferent hands. And now, tell me how I am going to manage to live." Always equal to her sister's need, Bronya did.

She sent Marie a Polish governess, both a practical and spiritual help. As Marie struggled to cope with her loss, the governess both watched her children and comforted her spirit—the daily reminder of Marie's homeland provided consolation her now-absent sister couldn't. And Marie did manage to live.

> *A ministering angel shall my sister be.*
>
> WILLIAM SHAKESPEARE

Five years later Bronya accompanied Marie to accept her second Nobel prize (she'd won the first with

Pierre). Marie enjoyed friendship with Albert Einstein. She continued her research. She saw to the building of the finely appointed laboratory Pierre had dreamed of. She participated heartily in the war effort, providing X-ray machines wherever needed. And she raised two children—one of whom earned a Nobel prize, the other who crafted a heartfelt biography of her famous mother.

Through it all, Bronya was there. If not in presence, in letters, in surprise visits, in their shared heart. When at last Marie joined Pierre in death, Bronya brought a handful of Polish soil to deposit on her grave. Their mutual love for their homeland bound them together, and neither would say the losses—long separations, exhausting work, grief—weren't worth it all.

I cannot deny that, now I am without your company I feel not only that I am deprived of a very dear sister, but that I have lost half of myself.

BEATRICE D'ESTE

Oh, the comfort—the inexpressible comfort
of feeling safe with a person,
Having neither to weigh thoughts,
Nor measure words—but pouring them
All right out—just as they are—
Chaff and grain together—
Certain that a faithful hand will
Take and sift them—
Keep what is worth keeping—
And with the breath of kindness
Blow the rest away.

DINAH MARIA
MULOCK CRAIK

*I*n these stories we have seen the immeasurable
influence of a sister. She forms the wall between one
and despair, and fills the balloons when celebration
comes. She is the friendliest friend, the deepest
connection, the most understanding ear. She is
the sense of home one never loses.

What greater thing is there for human souls than to feel that they are joined for life—to be with each other in silent unspeakable memories.

GEORGE ELIOT